Biotech Trading

Specialize in trading stocks of biotechnology companies based on drug development news and events

monetary loss due to the information herein, either directly or indirectly.

Respective authors own all copyrights not held by the publisher. The information herein is offered for informational purposes solely and is universal as such. The presentation of the data is without a contract or any guarantee assurance.

TABLE OF CONTENTS

Introduction:

The confluence of biotechnology and financial markets has given rise to a distinct realm of investment that demands both scientific acumen and financial expertise. In the intricate world of biotech trading, where the fortunes of companies are inexorably linked to the progress of drug development, mastery of technical analysis and an understanding of scientific breakthroughs become paramount. This book, "Biotech Trading: Navigating Biotechnology Stock Markets through Drug Development Insights," embarks on a journey through this dynamic landscape, unraveling the complexities that underlie successful trading within the biotech sector.

At its core, biotech trading is a symbiotic relationship between the intricate processes of drug discovery, development, and regulatory approval, and the fervent pulse of the financial markets. As investors navigate this arena, it's crucial to recognize the intertwined nature of scientific progress and market dynamics. A grasp of the phases of drug development—ranging from preclinical trials to post-marketing surveillance—equips traders with the knowledge to gauge the value potential of biotech stocks.

Biotechnology, an industry born from the confluence of biology, chemistry, and technology, continues to evolve at an astonishing pace. The first chapter of this book delves into the historical trajectory of the biotech sector, examining how it has evolved from its humble beginnings to becoming a pivotal player in modern healthcare. Understanding this evolution is essential, as historical patterns often foreshadow future trends, and recognizing these patterns is crucial for effective decision-making.

The second chapter is a deep dive into the fundamental intricacies of drug development—

an endeavor that epitomizes the intersection of science and commerce. The drug development lifecycle comprises a sequence of stages, each laden with its own unique challenges and critical milestones. From identifying promising drug candidates to navigating the rigorous landscape of clinical trials, an exhaustive comprehension of this lifecycle is imperative for investors looking to time their trades to maximize profit potential.

With clinical trials at the heart of drug development, the third chapter delves into the art and science of interpreting clinical trial results. A nuanced understanding of trial data—whether positive or negative—can spell the difference between lucrative returns and substantial losses. This chapter will empower traders to decipher complex trial data, ascertain its implications, and strategize their investments accordingly.

The regulatory framework governing biotech companies is as intricate as the science behind their innovations. Chapter four is dedicated to elucidating the labyrinthine corridors of the Food and Drug Administration (FDA) and the regulatory environment. Discerning the regulatory climate, comprehending approval processes, and anticipating market reactions to regulatory changes will equip traders with a tactical edge in this high-stakes arena.

As biotech trading entails a comprehensive assessment of companies' drug pipelines, chapter five provides an in-depth exploration of pipeline analysis. Evaluating the prospects of drugs in various stages of development, gauging their potential market impact, and weighing inherent risks are fundamental skills that this chapter imparts to traders.

In continuation, the next chapter delves into the intricate art of valuing biotech companies.

Traditional valuation metrics must be complemented with biotech-specific factors, such as the potential of pending clinical trials and regulatory approvals. This chapter equips traders with the prowess to assess companies' worth not just in terms of financials but also in terms of future catalysts.

Stay tuned as we delve into chapter seven, where we explore the enigmatic realm of market sentiment and investor behavior. The psychology that underpins the actions of biotech stock investors can significantly influence market movements. By understanding how news, rumors, and sentiment shape the market, traders can position themselves strategically, capitalizing on trends that others might overlook.

As we journey deeper into the book, subsequent chapters will explore event-driven trading strategies, risk management tactics, the role of exchange-traded funds (ETFs) and mutual funds in the biotech sector, and the intricate dance between intellectual property and stock performance. The pages that follow will weave real-life case studies, unveil data sources and research tools, and examine the ethical considerations that underscore biotech trading decisions.

In conclusion, this book is poised to be an indispensable resource for both novice and seasoned traders alike, offering a comprehensive guide to navigating the complex realm of biotech trading. Armed with scientific insights, financial acumen, and a robust arsenal of strategies, readers will be empowered to traverse the biotech stock markets with a newfound confidence. Stay tuned for the subsequent chapters that will pave the way to becoming a proficient biotech trader.

Chapter 1: Understanding Biotechnology Landscape

The first chapter of "Biotech Trading: Navigating Biotechnology Stock Markets through Drug Development Insights" immerses readers in the historical and contemporary dimensions of the biotechnology landscape. This foundational exploration is crucial for establishing a robust understanding of the context in which biotech trading operates.

Evolution of Biotech Industry: The biotechnology industry has undergone a remarkable transformation since its inception. Tracing its roots back to the recombinant DNA revolution of the 1970s, the industry has evolved from a nascent scientific pursuit to a global economic powerhouse. This chapter delves into the pioneering breakthroughs that marked the industry's inception, such as the development of recombinant insulin and the birth of genetic engineering. It then navigates through subsequent milestones, including the decoding of the human genome and the emergence of gene editing technologies like CRISPR-Cas9. By comprehending the trajectory of biotech advancements, traders can discern patterns that influence stock movements.

Key Players and Market Dynamics: A comprehensive understanding of the key players within the biotech sector is vital for effective trading. This chapter introduces readers to the array of stakeholders, from established pharmaceutical giants to agile startups. It scrutinizes the role of academia and research institutions in driving innovation, as well as the significance of venture capital in nurturing fledgling biotech ventures. Understanding the dynamics between large-cap companies and innovative startups is pivotal for predicting market trends. By dissecting the strategies of market leaders, traders can glean insights into potential winners and losers.

Market Sentiment and Investor Behavior in Biotech: Biotech trading is profoundly influenced by market sentiment and investor behavior. This chapter delves into the psychological underpinnings that drive investment decisions within the sector. Traders will explore how news, clinical trial results, and regulatory announcements can trigger euphoria or panic, leading to rapid stock fluctuations. By analyzing historical trends in investor sentiment, traders can develop a nuanced perspective on market behavior, allowing them to anticipate and adapt to market swings effectively.

Emerging Trends and Technological Disruptions: Innovation is the lifeblood of the biotech industry, and technological disruptions are pivotal in shaping market trends. This chapter examines cutting-edge advancements, such as precision medicine, immuno-oncology, and gene therapies. These trends can spark revolutionary changes in treatment paradigms, thus impacting the valuation of biotech companies. By staying attuned to emerging technologies, traders can position themselves to harness early-mover advantages, capitalizing on market movements driven by scientific breakthroughs.

Investment Strategies Based on Industry Evolution: Investment strategies within the biotech sector are inherently linked to the industry's evolution. This chapter guides readers in formulating strategies based on the lifecycle of biotechnology companies. Traders will learn to recognize opportunities for early-stage investments in startups with disruptive technologies, mid-stage investments as drugs progress through clinical trials, and late-stage investments in companies approaching regulatory approvals. Tailoring investment strategies to match the stages of company development can yield substantial returns and mitigate risk.

As readers navigate through the pages of this chapter, they will gain a comprehensive understanding of the biotechnology landscape's historical context, market dynamics, and the interplay between innovation and investment. Armed with this knowledge, traders can build a solid foundation for their journey into the intricate world of biotech trading, poised to make informed decisions that yield both financial success and a deeper appreciation for the fusion of science and finance.

Chapter 2: Fundamentals of Drug Development

In the intricate tapestry of biotech trading, a profound comprehension of the fundamental processes underlying drug development is essential. Chapter 2 of "Biotech Trading: Navigating Biotechnology Stock Markets through Drug Development Insights" delves into the multi-phased journey of drug development, providing readers with the tools to decode this intricate landscape and make informed trading decisions.

Phases of Drug Development: The chapter initiates with a meticulous exploration of the phases that constitute the drug development pipeline. From preclinical research to post-marketing surveillance, each phase presents unique challenges and potential market impacts. Readers will glean insights into the sequential progression of drug candidates through phases such as discovery, preclinical testing, clinical trials, and regulatory approval. By understanding these stages, traders can anticipate pivotal milestones that can catalyze stock movements.

Clinical Trials: A Crucial Crucible: At the heart of drug development lie clinical trials—a pivotal juncture where scientific rigor converges with regulatory scrutiny. This chapter delves into the intricate design and execution of clinical trials, deciphering the significance of randomized controlled trials, double-blind studies, and placebo controls. Readers will learn how to interpret clinical trial protocols, data, and endpoints, enabling them to assess the potential success or failure of investigational drugs and make informed trading choices.

Challenges and Regulatory Hurdles: Navigating the labyrinthine regulatory landscape is a defining challenge in drug development. This chapter dissects the role of regulatory bodies such as the FDA and EMA, shedding light on the stringent standards that govern drug approvals. Readers will delve into topics such as orphan drug designations, fast-track programs, and breakthrough therapy designations, which can expedite the approval process for certain drugs. Understanding the regulatory pathways and potential hurdles equips traders to anticipate market reactions to regulatory updates.

Understanding Clinical Data: Clinical trial data, replete with its complexities and nuances, forms the bedrock of investment decisions in the biotech sector. This chapter equips traders with the analytical tools to discern the significance of trial data. From endpoints and statistical significance to adverse events and patient populations, readers will unravel the intricacies that underlie clinical data interpretation. Armed with this knowledge, traders can differentiate between meaningful breakthroughs and transient fluctuations.

Market Implications of Drug Development Phases: The chapter culminates with an exploration of how different phases of drug development impact stock performance. Traders will delve into case studies and historical data to discern patterns in market behavior corresponding to specific developmental milestones. Whether it's the euphoria surrounding positive clinical trial results or the skepticism accompanying regulatory setbacks, understanding the interplay between science and market sentiment is pivotal for maximizing trading outcomes.

In navigating through the corridors of this chapter, readers will emerge equipped with a comprehensive understanding of the intricate landscape of drug development. Armed with insights into the phases, challenges, and implications of drug development, traders will be better poised to anticipate market movements, capitalize on pivotal events, and make judicious trading decisions. As the curtain rises on the next chapters, readers will be primed to delve even deeper into the multifaceted realm of biotech trading.

Chapter 3: Analyzing Clinical Trial Results

Within the realm of biotech trading, the ability to decipher and analyze clinical trial results is a critical skill that sets successful traders apart. Chapter 3 of "Biotech Trading: Navigating Biotechnology Stock Markets through Drug Development Insights" delves into the intricate world of clinical trial data interpretation, empowering readers to discern the scientific and market implications of trial outcomes.

Interpreting Trial Data for Investment Decisions: This chapter commences by illuminating the pivotal role of clinical trial results in shaping investment decisions. Traders will delve into the various types of trial data, such as efficacy, safety, and secondary endpoints, and learn how to assess their significance in the context of drug development. Through real-world case studies, readers will gain insights into how different trial outcomes can impact stock prices and market sentiment.

Impact of Positive and Negative Outcomes: The heart of clinical trial analysis lies in comprehending the implications of positive and negative outcomes. This chapter dissects the market dynamics that unfold when a drug candidate demonstrates efficacy, safety, and other desired attributes. Conversely, it explores how setbacks and adverse outcomes can trigger rapid market reactions. By understanding the intricate interplay between clinical trial data and stock movement, traders can position themselves strategically to capitalize on market volatility.

Biostatistics and Data Integrity: A deep dive into clinical trial data necessitates an understanding of biostatistics and the intricacies of data integrity. This chapter introduces readers to statistical concepts such as p-values, confidence intervals, and statistical significance. It also explores factors that can influence data quality and integrity, such as patient demographics, trial design, and randomization techniques. Armed with this knowledge, traders can critically assess the reliability of trial results and make informed judgments.

Endpoints and Their Relevance: The choice of clinical trial endpoints profoundly influences the interpretation of trial data. This chapter examines different types of endpoints, such as primary, secondary, and exploratory endpoints, and their relevance in assessing the success of drug candidates. Traders will learn how to discern meaningful clinical outcomes from surrogate endpoints, enhancing their ability to differentiate between substantial therapeutic advances and superficial statistical variations.

Balancing Data and Market Expectations: Balancing scientific rigor with market expectations is a delicate task in biotech trading. This chapter delves into how market sentiment can sometimes outpace the underlying clinical evidence, leading to stock movements that may not align with the true therapeutic value of a drug candidate. Readers will acquire the acumen to critically evaluate the alignment between trial data and market reactions, enabling them to make well-informed trading choices.

By journeying through the pages of this chapter, traders and enthusiasts alike will be equipped with the analytical tools to navigate the intricate landscape of clinical trial data interpretation. Armed with insights into positive and negative outcomes, an understanding of biostatistics, and an appreciation for the interplay between data and market sentiment, readers will be primed to make astute trading decisions based on a nuanced comprehension of clinical trial results. As the book unfolds, subsequent chapters will further refine the skill set necessary for successful biotech trading.

Chapter 4: FDA and Regulatory Landscape

In the dynamic world of biotech trading, the regulatory landscape plays a pivotal role in influencing stock movements and investment decisions. Chapter 4 of "Biotech Trading: Navigating Biotechnology Stock Markets through Drug Development Insights" delves into the intricacies of the Food and Drug Administration (FDA) and the broader regulatory environment, equipping readers with the knowledge to anticipate and navigate regulatory changes.

Navigating FDA Approvals and Regulations: This chapter commences by unraveling the role of the FDA as a gatekeeper for drug approvals in the United States. Traders will gain insights into the stages of FDA review, from Investigational New Drug (IND) application to New Drug Application (NDA) submission. By understanding the regulatory processes and timelines, traders can strategically position themselves to capitalize on potential market movements triggered by FDA decisions.

Market Response to Regulatory Updates: Regulatory decisions and updates can send ripples through the biotech stock market. This chapter delves into how the market responds to FDA approvals, rejections, and safety advisories. By examining historical examples, readers will grasp the patterns of market behavior that follow regulatory announcements. Armed with this knowledge, traders can navigate the volatility that often accompanies such updates and make informed trading choices.

Accelerated Pathways and Fast-Track Programs: The FDA offers several accelerated pathways and fast-track programs to expedite the development and approval of drugs for serious conditions. This chapter dissects these programs, such as the Breakthrough Therapy Designation and the Priority Review, exploring how they can influence stock performance. Readers will learn to discern the implications of these designations for both scientific progress and market sentiment.

Regulatory Challenges and Their Market Impact: The regulatory journey is not devoid of challenges, including safety concerns, label restrictions, and post-marketing surveillance. This chapter delves into how regulatory hurdles can impact stock performance. Traders will gain insights into the market's reaction to adverse events, label changes, and regulatory actions. By assessing the potential market reverberations of regulatory challenges, traders can make calculated decisions amid uncertainties.

Global Regulatory Variations: The regulatory landscape extends beyond the borders of the United States. This chapter examines how regulatory agencies in different countries impact biotech stock trading. Traders will explore the European Medicines Agency (EMA), the Pharmaceuticals and Medical Devices Agency (PMDA) in Japan, and other international regulatory bodies. Understanding global regulatory variations equips traders to anticipate worldwide market trends.

As readers immerse themselves in the intricacies of this chapter, they will gain a comprehensive understanding of how the FDA and regulatory dynamics intertwine with the biotech trading landscape. Armed with insights into navigating FDA approvals, interpreting market responses to regulatory updates, and understanding the impact of fast-track programs, traders will be primed to navigate the ever-evolving regulatory environment with acumen and confidence. As the chapters unfold, subsequent sections will continue to expand the horizons of biotech trading expertise.

Chapter 5: Assessing Pipeline Potential

The success of biotech trading hinges on the ability to discern the potential of drug pipelines within biotechnology companies. Chapter 5 of "Biotech Trading: Navigating Biotechnology Stock Markets through Drug Development Insights" immerses readers into the intricate art of pipeline analysis, equipping them to assess investment opportunities with a discerning eye.

Evaluating Company Pipelines as Investment Opportunities: This chapter embarks by highlighting the significance of evaluating biotech company pipelines as a cornerstone of investment decisions. Traders will delve into the diverse stages of drug development—ranging from preclinical to post-marketing—and understand how each phase contributes to a company's value. By discerning the mix of early-stage exploratory drugs and late-stage candidates, readers can gauge a company's growth potential.

Balancing Risk and Reward: Pipeline analysis necessitates a careful balance between risk and reward. This chapter dissects the factors that contribute to risk within drug pipelines, such as clinical trial failures, regulatory setbacks, and market dynamics. Traders will learn how to assess the inherent risk in different stages of drug development and make informed judgments about potential rewards. By understanding this delicate equilibrium, readers can formulate strategies to manage risk effectively.

Impact of Pipeline Diversity: Diversity within a drug pipeline can be a pivotal indicator of a company's resilience and growth potential. This chapter delves into the value of having a diversified pipeline that spans therapeutic areas and mechanisms of action. Traders will explore how having multiple candidates targeting different indications can mitigate the impact of setbacks and enhance a company's long-term prospects.

Valuing Development Milestones: As drug candidates progress through development stages, reaching critical milestones becomes a marker of progress. This chapter guides readers in understanding the significance of development milestones, such as successful completion of clinical phases or regulatory designations. Traders will learn how to assign value to these milestones, factoring them into their investment assessments to predict potential stock movements.

Anticipating Catalysts and Value Inflection Points: Pipeline analysis involves anticipating catalysts—events that can significantly impact a company's stock price and valuation. This chapter examines catalysts such as clinical trial results, regulatory decisions, and partnership agreements. Traders will gain insights into how to identify upcoming catalysts, assess their potential market impact, and position themselves strategically to capitalize on value inflection points.

As readers navigate the depths of this chapter, they will emerge equipped with the analytical tools necessary to assess pipeline potential within the biotech sector. By understanding the nuances of pipeline evaluation, balancing risk and reward, recognizing the impact of pipeline diversity, valuing development milestones, and anticipating value-inflection catalysts, traders will be poised to make astute investment decisions that are grounded in a comprehensive comprehension of a company's growth trajectory. The journey through the intricate terrain of biotech trading continues to unfold in subsequent chapters, providing readers with an arsenal of insights and strategies.

Chapter 6: Biotech Valuation Techniques

Valuation within the biotech sector is a unique blend of financial analysis and scientific potential. Chapter 6 of "Biotech Trading: Navigating Biotechnology Stock Markets through Drug Development Insights" delves into the intricacies of valuing biotech companies, equipping readers with the skills to assess both financial metrics and the developmental milestones that drive stock prices.

Traditional Metrics vs. Biotech-Specific Valuation: This chapter initiates by dissecting the traditional valuation metrics commonly used in the financial world. Traders will explore metrics like price-to-earnings (P/E) ratios, price-to-sales (P/S) ratios, and discounted cash flow (DCF) models. However, valuing biotech companies extends beyond these metrics. The chapter guides readers in understanding how to integrate biotech-specific factors such as clinical trial progress, regulatory milestones, and pipeline potential into their valuation strategies.

Incorporating Development Milestones in Valuation: The incorporation of developmental milestones is a hallmark of biotech valuation. This chapter delves into how traders can assign value to clinical trial successes, regulatory designations, and other pivotal milestones. By estimating the impact of these milestones on a company's valuation, traders can make informed decisions that reflect the potential for future growth.

Patent and Intellectual Property Valuation: Intellectual property and patents are integral to a biotech company's valuation. This chapter examines how to assess the value of a company's intellectual property portfolio, including patents, licenses, and proprietary technologies. Traders will gain insights into how patent expiration and exclusivity impact stock performance and how to factor these elements into their valuation models.

Calculating Market Potential and Revenue Forecasts: Understanding a drug candidate's market potential and revenue forecasts is crucial for accurate valuation. This chapter guides readers in assessing the target patient population, pricing strategies, and potential market share. By incorporating these factors into their valuation models, traders can project future revenue streams and estimate a company's growth trajectory.

Evaluating Partnerhips and Collaborations: Partnerships and collaborations can significantly impact a biotech company's valuation. This chapter explores how strategic alliances, licensing agreements, and partnerships can enhance a company's financial prospects. Traders will learn to assess the financial and developmental implications of these collaborations and incorporate them into their valuation assessments.

As readers immerse themselves in this chapter, they will emerge equipped with the analytical prowess to navigate the intricate landscape of biotech valuation. By understanding the interplay between traditional financial metrics and biotech-specific factors, incorporating developmental milestones, valuing intellectual property, forecasting market potential, and evaluating partnerships, traders will be poised to make well-informed trading decisions that are grounded in a holistic understanding of a company's value. The journey through the world of biotech trading continues, with subsequent chapters delving even deeper into specialized insights and strategies.

Chapter 7: Market Sentiment and Investor Behavior

In the dynamic world of biotech trading, market sentiment and investor behavior wield significant influence over stock movements. Chapter 7 of "Biotech Trading: Navigating Biotechnology Stock Markets through Drug Development Insights" delves into the psychological underpinnings that drive trading decisions and explores how news, rumors, and speculation shape market sentiment.

Psychology of Biotech Stock Investors: This chapter commences by unraveling the intricate psychology that underpins trading decisions within the biotech sector. Traders will delve into cognitive biases, herd behavior, and risk perception that can lead to market trends and price fluctuations. By understanding the psychological factors that influence investor behavior, traders can anticipate market movements and position themselves strategically.

Impact of News and Speculation: News, whether substantiated or speculative, can trigger rapid market reactions in the biotech sector. This chapter examines how news about clinical trial results, regulatory approvals, partnerships, and scientific breakthroughs can propel stocks to new heights or precipitate sharp declines. Readers will learn to distinguish between credible information and baseless rumors, and gauge their impact on market sentiment.

Event-Driven Trading and Timing: Event-driven trading strategies hinge on capitalizing on news-driven price movements. This chapter explores the intricacies of timing trades around events such as FDA announcements, clinical trial readouts, and major conferences. Traders will gain insights into how to anticipate market sentiment shifts, enter positions strategically, and exit at optimal points to maximize trading outcomes.

Behavioral Biases and Their Market Impact: Behavioral biases, ranging from fear of missing out (FOMO) to loss aversion, can drive irrational trading behavior. This chapter dissects these biases and their implications for stock movements. By understanding how these biases can lead to overvaluation or undervaluation of stocks, traders can make informed decisions that capitalize on market inefficiencies.

Role of Social Media and Online Forums: The advent of social media and online forums has amplified the impact of retail investors on the stock market. This chapter examines how platforms like Twitter, Reddit, and stock-focused forums can amplify sentiment shifts and drive stock prices. Traders will learn to gauge the influence of online communities and assess the reliability of information circulating on these platforms.

As readers immerse themselves in this chapter, they will emerge equipped with a nuanced understanding of market sentiment and investor behavior within the biotech sector. By delving into the psychology of investors, exploring the impact of news and speculation, mastering event-driven trading strategies, understanding the role of behavioral biases, and navigating the influence of social media, traders will be primed to anticipate and capitalize on the complex interplay between psychology and market dynamics. As subsequent chapters unfold, readers will delve even deeper into the multifaceted world of biotech trading expertise.

Chapter 8: Event-Driven Trading Strategies

Event-driven trading strategies are a cornerstone of success in biotech trading, where market movements are often catalyzed by significant announcements and milestones. Chapter 8 of "Biotech Trading: Navigating Biotechnology Stock Markets through Drug Development Insights" delves into the art of leveraging critical events to make strategic trading decisions.

Leveraging FDA Announcements and Clinical Trial Milestones: This chapter commences by highlighting the significance of FDA announcements and clinical trial milestones as potent catalysts for stock movements. Traders will explore how FDA decisions, such as drug approvals and rejections, can trigger rapid price shifts. Likewise, they will learn to anticipate the impact of clinical trial results on a company's valuation and stock performance.

Timing Entries and Exits: Effective event-driven trading hinges on precise timing of market entries and exits. This chapter dissects the strategies for entering positions ahead of anticipated positive news and exiting before potential negative outcomes. Traders will learn how to strike a balance between maximizing potential gains and mitigating risks, all while navigating the inherent volatility associated with event-driven trading.

Analyzing Market Reaction Patterns: Past market reactions to similar events can offer invaluable insights for future trading decisions. This chapter guides readers in analyzing historical data to discern patterns in market reactions. By understanding how stocks tend to respond to specific types of news, traders can refine their strategies and make well-informed decisions based on empirical evidence.

Using Options and Derivatives for Event-Driven Trades: Options and derivatives can enhance the efficacy of event-driven trading strategies. This chapter explores how traders can leverage options to capitalize on anticipated price movements and hedge against potential losses. Readers will learn to construct option strategies that align with their trading outlook and risk tolerance.

Adapting to Unexpected Outcomes: While event-driven trading is based on anticipation, unexpected outcomes can still arise. This chapter examines how to adapt to unexpected news and market movements. Traders will gain insights into risk management strategies that allow them to respond swiftly and strategically to unforeseen events.

As readers navigate the depths of this chapter, they will emerge equipped with the tools and tactics necessary to excel in event-driven trading within the biotech sector. By leveraging FDA announcements, mastering the timing of market entries and exits, analyzing market reaction patterns, exploring options and derivatives, and adapting to unexpected outcomes, traders will be primed to capitalize on the dynamic landscape of event-driven trading. As subsequent chapters unfold, readers will continue to refine their expertise in biotech trading strategies.

Chapter 9: Risk Management in Biotech Trading

Effective risk management is a linchpin of success in the volatile realm of biotech trading. Chapter 9 of "Biotech Trading: Navigating Biotechnology Stock Markets through Drug Development Insights" delves into strategies for mitigating risks and safeguarding investments in a sector characterized by rapid market swings and uncertainty.

Understanding Biotech-Specific Risks: This chapter initiates by dissecting the unique risks inherent to biotech trading. Traders will explore factors such as clinical trial failures, regulatory setbacks, and competitive landscape shifts that can trigger sharp stock declines. By understanding these biotech-specific risks, traders can proactively manage their portfolios and make informed trading decisions.

Diversification and Portfolio Allocation: Diversification is a cornerstone of effective risk management. This chapter delves into strategies for diversifying a biotech trading portfolio across different companies, therapeutic areas, and stages of development. Traders will learn how to allocate capital strategically to manage risk while still capitalizing on potential opportunities.

Hedging Techniques and Risk Mitigation: Hedging is an essential tool for mitigating risks in a volatile market. This chapter explores how options and derivatives can be used to hedge against potential losses due to adverse market movements. Traders will gain insights into constructing hedging strategies that align with their trading objectives and risk tolerance.

Position Sizing and Risk-Reward Ratios: Proper position sizing is critical for managing risk effectively. This chapter guides traders in determining the appropriate size of their positions based on their risk tolerance and trading strategy. Readers will learn to calculate risk-reward ratios and assess the potential returns against the inherent risks of their trades.

Monitoring and Adjusting Risk Strategies: Risk management is an ongoing process that requires vigilance and adaptation. This chapter examines how to monitor portfolio performance, assess risk exposure, and adjust risk strategies as market conditions evolve. Traders will gain insights into staying agile and making prudent adjustments to manage risk effectively.

As readers delve into the depths of this chapter, they will emerge equipped with the tools and techniques necessary to navigate the intricate landscape of risk management within biotech trading. By understanding biotech-specific risks, diversifying portfolios, employing hedging techniques, sizing positions effectively, and maintaining an adaptive risk strategy, traders will be primed to navigate the volatility of the biotech sector with resilience and confidence. As the book unfolds, subsequent chapters will continue to refine and expand on the art of successful biotech trading.

Chapter 10: Biotech ETFs and Funds

Exchange-Traded Funds (ETFs) and mutual funds offer investors a diversified exposure to the biotech sector, mitigating individual stock risks. Chapter 10 of "Biotech Trading: Navigating Biotechnology Stock Markets through Drug Development Insights" explores the benefits, drawbacks, and strategies associated with investing in these vehicles.

Understanding Biotech ETFs and Funds: This chapter commences by introducing readers to the concept of biotech ETFs and mutual funds. Traders will gain insights into how these investment vehicles pool resources from multiple investors to invest in a diversified portfolio of biotech stocks. By understanding the structure and mechanics of ETFs and funds, traders can explore different avenues for exposure to the biotech sector.

Benefits of Diversification and Risk Mitigation: Diversification is a hallmark of ETFs and funds, offering inherent risk mitigation. This chapter delves into how investing in these vehicles can reduce the impact of individual stock fluctuations and provide exposure to a broader range of biotech companies. Traders will explore how diversification can enhance portfolio stability and align with their risk tolerance.

Performance Evaluation and Selection Criteria: Selecting the right biotech ETFs or funds is pivotal for successful investment. This chapter guides readers in evaluating the performance of different funds by analyzing historical returns, expense ratios, and other relevant metrics. Traders will learn how to assess the alignment of a fund's investment strategy with their own trading objectives.

Tracking Indices and Sectors: Many biotech ETFs and funds track specific indices or sectors within the biotech industry. This chapter explores how different indices, such as the NASDAQ Biotechnology Index, can influence fund performance. Traders will gain insights into how tracking specific indices can align with their market outlook and investment preferences.

Potential Drawbacks and Considerations: While ETFs and funds offer diversification, they also come with potential drawbacks. This chapter examines factors such as management fees, tracking error, and tax implications associated with these investment vehicles. By understanding these considerations, traders can make informed decisions about incorporating ETFs and funds into their portfolio.

As readers immerse themselves in the intricacies of this chapter, they will emerge equipped with the insights necessary to explore the world of biotech ETFs and funds. By understanding the benefits of diversification, evaluating performance and selection criteria, tracking relevant indices, and considering potential drawbacks, traders will be poised to diversify their investment strategies and leverage these vehicles to gain exposure to the biotech sector. The journey through the landscape of biotech trading continues, with subsequent chapters further refining and expanding on investment opportunities and strategies

Chapter 11: Analyzing Intellectual Property

Intellectual property (IP) plays a pivotal role in shaping the biotech sector and influencing stock performance. Chapter 11 of "Biotech Trading: Navigating Biotechnology Stock Markets through Drug Development Insights" delves into the intricacies of patents, trademarks, and other forms of IP, equipping readers to assess their impact on market sentiment and investment decisions.

Role of Intellectual Property in Biotech: This chapter commences by highlighting the central role of intellectual property in the biotech industry. Traders will explore how patents and other forms of IP protect the innovative discoveries and technologies that underlie biotech companies' products. By understanding how IP can confer competitive advantages, traders can gauge its influence on stock valuations.

Analyzing Patent Portfolios: Patents are a key indicator of a biotech company's innovative prowess and potential market value. This chapter guides readers in evaluating patent portfolios to discern the breadth, depth, and quality of a company's intellectual property. Traders will explore how to assess the strength of patents, their coverage, and their potential to safeguard a company's competitive position.

Patent Exclusivity and Market Dynamics: Patent exclusivity grants biotech companies a window of market exclusivity for their products. This chapter examines how patent expiration can impact stock performance, leading to market shifts known as the "patent cliff." Traders will gain insights into how to anticipate the expiration of key patents and its potential repercussions on stock prices.

IP Litigation and Regulatory Considerations: IP litigation and regulatory challenges can introduce uncertainties in the biotech sector. This chapter delves into how legal battles over patents and regulatory hurdles can impact stock movements. Traders will learn to assess the potential outcomes of IP disputes and regulatory actions, and their implications for market sentiment.

Market Reaction to IP Developments: Market sentiment can be influenced by significant IP developments such as patent grants, rejections, and licensing agreements. This chapter explores how traders can anticipate market reactions to these events, using IP-related news to inform their trading decisions. By understanding how IP developments can sway investor sentiment, traders can position themselves strategically.

As readers navigate the depths of this chapter, they will emerge equipped with the analytical prowess necessary to navigate the complex landscape of intellectual property within the biotech sector. By understanding the role of IP in biotech, analyzing patent portfolios, anticipating patent exclusivity dynamics, considering IP litigation and regulatory challenges, and assessing market reactions to IP developments, traders will be primed to make informed investment decisions grounded in a comprehensive understanding of the intellectual property landscape. Subsequent chapters will continue to delve into specialized insights and strategies within biotech trading.

Chapter 12: Biotech Market Analysis and Data Sources

Effective biotech trading relies on accurate and timely market analysis. Chapter 12 of "Biotech Trading: Navigating Biotechnology Stock Markets through Drug Development Insights" delves into the tools, data sources, and analytical techniques that traders can leverage to gain insights into market trends, stock performance, and industry dynamics.

Data Sources for Biotech Analysis: This chapter commences by introducing readers to the diverse data sources available for biotech market analysis. Traders will explore platforms such as financial news websites, market research reports, clinical trial databases, regulatory agency websites, and scientific journals. By understanding the spectrum of data sources, traders can curate a comprehensive information repository.

Tracking News and Developments: Staying updated on news and developments is pivotal in biotech trading. This chapter guides readers in effectively tracking news related to clinical trial results, regulatory decisions, partnerships, and industry trends. Traders will learn how to differentiate between credible sources, assess the reliability of news, and use news feeds to inform their trading decisions.

Analyzing Clinical Trial Data: Clinical trial data is a treasure trove of information for biotech traders. This chapter examines how to access and interpret clinical trial data from sources like clinicaltrials.gov and scientific publications. Traders will learn to analyze trial protocols, endpoints, patient populations, and statistical data to gain insights into a drug candidate's potential.

Utilizing Market Research Reports: Market research reports provide comprehensive insights into industry trends, competitive landscapes, and future forecasts. This chapter explores how to leverage market research reports to assess market potential, identify emerging trends, and evaluate the competitive positioning of biotech companies. Traders will gain insights into using these reports to inform their investment decisions.

Technical Analysis in Biotech Trading: Technical analysis involves studying historical stock price patterns and trading volumes to forecast future price movements. This chapter examines how traders can use technical analysis tools such as moving averages, support and resistance levels, and chart patterns to gauge market sentiment and make trading decisions.

As readers immerse themselves in this chapter, they will emerge equipped with the tools and techniques necessary to perform comprehensive biotech market analysis. By understanding data sources, tracking news and developments, analyzing clinical trial data, utilizing market research reports, and exploring technical analysis tools, traders will be poised to make informed trading decisions based on a solid foundation of market insights. As the journey through the world of biotech trading unfolds, subsequent chapters will continue to expand on specialized strategies and insights.

Chapter 13: Long-Term Investing in Biotech

While biotech trading often involves short-term strategies, long-term investing can also yield substantial rewards in the sector. Chapter 13 of "Biotech Trading: Navigating Biotechnology Stock Markets through Drug Development Insights" delves into the considerations, strategies, and factors to bear in mind when adopting a long-term investment approach within the biotech industry.

Benefits and Challenges of Long-Term Investing: This chapter commences by exploring the benefits of adopting a long-term investment strategy within the biotech sector. Traders will examine how a patient approach can capitalize on the potential for drug candidates to progress through clinical stages and achieve regulatory approvals. Additionally, the chapter will address the challenges associated with long-term investing, such as market volatility and the inherent uncertainties in drug development.

Assessing Developmental Milestones: Long-term investing in biotech requires a keen understanding of developmental milestones. This chapter guides readers in assessing the significance of milestones such as Phase 1, 2, and 3 clinical trial results, FDA approvals, and commercial launches. Traders will learn how to gauge the potential impact of these milestones on a company's valuation and stock performance.

Balancing Portfolio for Long-Term Growth: Diversification is paramount for long-term growth. This chapter delves into strategies for balancing a portfolio of biotech stocks across different stages of development, therapeutic areas, and market caps. Traders will explore how to create a diversified portfolio that aligns with their long-term investment objectives while managing risk effectively.

Evaluating Management and Leadership: In the realm of long-term investing, assessing a company's management and leadership becomes pivotal. This chapter examines how to evaluate a company's management team, their track record, and their ability to execute on their developmental goals. Traders will learn to factor management competence into their investment decisions.

Understanding Biotech Market Cycles: Biotech stocks often experience cycles of euphoria and pessimism. This chapter explores how to navigate these market cycles while adhering to a long-term investment strategy. Traders will gain insights into recognizing when market sentiment overshoots or undershoots the underlying value of a company, enabling them to capitalize on market inefficiencies.

As readers immerse themselves in the intricacies of this chapter, they will emerge equipped with the insights necessary to thrive in long-term investing within the biotech sector. By understanding the benefits and challenges of long-term strategies, assessing developmental milestones, balancing portfolios for growth, evaluating management and leadership, and navigating market cycles, traders will be poised to capitalize on the potential for sustained growth and value creation. The journey through the realm of biotech trading continues, with subsequent chapters further refining and expanding on investment strategies and expertise.

Chapter 14: Ethical Considerations in Biotech Trading

Ethical considerations are pivotal in navigating the biotech trading landscape, where decisions can impact human health and well-being. Chapter 14 of "Biotech Trading: Navigating Biotechnology Stock Markets through Drug Development Insights" delves into the ethical dilemmas, responsibilities, and considerations that traders should bear in mind when engaging in biotech trading.

Balancing Profit and Ethical Responsibility: This chapter commences by examining the delicate balance between pursuing profit and upholding ethical responsibilities. Traders will explore the ethical implications of trading in stocks tied to life-saving therapies and groundbreaking medical advancements. By understanding the gravity of their actions, traders can make decisions that align with their personal values and broader ethical considerations.

Clinical Trial Ethics and Patient Well-Being: The conduct of clinical trials raises ethical concerns, as patient safety and well-being are paramount. This chapter delves into how traders can evaluate companies' commitment to ethical clinical trial practices. Traders will learn to assess transparency, patient consent, and adherence to ethical standards when considering investment opportunities.

Responsible Use of Information: Traders often have access to non-public information that can impact stock prices. This chapter explores the ethical implications of using confidential information to gain an unfair advantage. Traders will gain insights into insider trading regulations and the importance of conducting trades based on publicly available information.

Environmental and Social Responsibility: Biotech companies are often engaged in research and development that can impact the environment and society. This chapter examines how traders can evaluate a company's environmental and social responsibility practices. Traders will learn to consider factors such as sustainability, diversity and inclusion, and corporate social responsibility when making investment decisions.

Promoting Ethical Practices: Traders have the potential to influence corporate behavior through their investment decisions. This chapter explores how traders can engage in responsible investing that encourages companies to prioritize ethical practices. Traders will learn to use their influence to promote transparency, accountability, and ethical behavior within the biotech sector.

As readers navigate the depths of this chapter, they will emerge equipped with the ethical compass necessary to navigate the complex ethical landscape of biotech trading. By balancing profit and ethical responsibility, considering clinical trial ethics, using information responsibly, evaluating environmental and social responsibility, and promoting ethical practices, traders will be primed to engage in biotech trading with integrity and mindfulness. The journey through the world of biotech trading continues, with subsequent chapters continuing to expand on specialized insights and strategies.

Chapter 14: Ethical Considerations in Biotech Trading

Ethical considerations are pivotal in navigating the biotech trading landscape, where decisions can impact human health and well-being. Chapter 14 of "Biotech Trading: Navigating Biotechnology Stock Markets through Drug Development Insights" delves into the ethical dilemmas, responsibilities, and considerations that traders should bear in mind when engaging in biotech trading.

Balancing Profit and Ethical Responsibility: This chapter commences by examining the delicate balance between pursuing profit and upholding ethical responsibilities. Traders will explore the ethical implications of trading in stocks tied to life-saving therapies and groundbreaking medical advancements. By understanding the gravity of their actions, traders can make decisions that align with their personal values and broader ethical considerations.

Clinical Trial Ethics and Patient Well-Being: The conduct of clinical trials raises ethical concerns, as patient safety and well-being are paramount. This chapter delves into how traders can evaluate companies' commitment to ethical clinical trial practices. Traders will learn to assess transparency, patient consent, and adherence to ethical standards when considering investment opportunities.

Responsible Use of Information: Traders often have access to non-public information that can impact stock prices. This chapter explores the ethical implications of using confidential information to gain an unfair advantage. Traders will gain insights into insider trading regulations and the importance of conducting trades based on publicly available information.

Environmental and Social Responsibility: Biotech companies are often engaged in research and development that can impact the environment and society. This chapter examines how traders can evaluate a company's environmental and social responsibility practices. Traders will learn to consider factors such as sustainability, diversity and inclusion, and corporate social responsibility when making investment decisions.

Promoting Ethical Practices: Traders have the potential to influence corporate behavior through their investment decisions. This chapter explores how traders can engage in responsible investing that encourages companies to prioritize ethical practices. Traders will learn to use their influence to promote transparency, accountability, and ethical behavior within the biotech sector.

As readers navigate the depths of this chapter, they will emerge equipped with the ethical compass necessary to navigate the complex ethical landscape of biotech trading. By balancing profit and ethical responsibility, considering clinical trial ethics, using information responsibly, evaluating environmental and social responsibility, and promoting ethical practices, traders will be primed to engage in biotech trading with integrity and mindfulness. The journey through the world of biotech trading continues, with subsequent chapters continuing to expand on specialized insights and strategies.

Chapter 15: Emerging Technologies and Trends

The biotech sector is shaped by rapidly evolving technologies and trends that can drive stock performance. Chapter 15 of "Biotech Trading: Navigating Biotechnology Stock Markets through Drug Development Insights" delves into the emerging technologies, trends, and innovations that traders should be attuned to when making investment decisions in the biotech industry.

Gene Editing and CRISPR Technology: This chapter commences by exploring the revolutionary field of gene editing and the CRISPR-Cas9 technology. Traders will gain insights into how gene editing techniques can be harnessed to develop innovative therapies and treatments. By understanding the potential of gene editing, traders can gauge the market impact of breakthroughs in this domain.

Precision Medicine and Personalized Therapies: Precision medicine tailors treatments to individual patient characteristics, revolutionizing healthcare. This chapter examines how personalized therapies are transforming the biotech landscape and influencing stock performance. Traders will explore how to assess companies that are at the forefront of developing targeted treatments.

Artificial Intelligence and Data Analytics: Artificial intelligence (AI) and data analytics are reshaping drug discovery, clinical trials, and market analysis. This chapter delves into the role of AI in identifying drug candidates, optimizing trial designs, and predicting market trends. Traders will learn to assess the potential impact of AI-driven innovations on companies' value and stock performance.

Biotech's Role in Pandemic Preparedness: Recent global health crises have underscored the importance of biotech in pandemic preparedness. This chapter examines how biotech companies contribute to vaccine development, antiviral treatments, and diagnostics. Traders will explore how pandemic-related developments can impact market sentiment and stock prices.

Sustainability and ESG Considerations: Environmental, social, and governance (ESG) considerations are gaining prominence in investment decisions. This chapter explores how biotech companies address sustainability, social responsibility, and ethical governance. Traders will learn to assess companies' ESG practices and evaluate their potential influence on stock performance.

As readers immerse themselves in the intricacies of this chapter, they will emerge equipped with insights into the cutting-edge technologies and trends shaping the biotech sector. By understanding the potential of gene editing, precision medicine, AI, pandemic preparedness, and ESG considerations, traders will be poised to identify investment opportunities driven by emerging technologies and trends. The journey through the realm of biotech trading continues, with subsequent chapters further refining and expanding on investment strategies and expertise.

Chapter 16: Case Studies in Biotech Trading

Real-world case studies provide valuable insights into the application of strategies and principles within the biotech trading landscape. Chapter 16 of "Biotech Trading: Navigating Biotechnology Stock Markets through Drug Development Insights" delves into a series of case studies that showcase successful and challenging trading scenarios, offering readers practical lessons and perspectives.

Case Study 1: The Breakthrough Designation Boost This chapter commences with a case study involving a biotech company that receives a Breakthrough Therapy Designation for one of its drug candidates. Traders will explore how this regulatory designation impacts stock performance, market sentiment, and trading decisions. By dissecting the key elements of this case, readers will learn to navigate opportunities presented by regulatory milestones.

Case Study 2: Clinical Trial Surprise In this case study, a biotech company's clinical trial results diverge from market expectations. Traders will delve into how unexpected outcomes can trigger volatility and impact stock prices. By analyzing the factors that contribute to the market's response, readers will gain insights into managing risks associated with clinical trial surprises.

Case Study 3: M&A and Strategic Partnerships This chapter explores a case study involving a merger and acquisition (M&A) deal between two biotech companies. Traders will examine how M&A announcements and strategic partnerships can reshape the biotech landscape and trigger stock movements. By evaluating the dynamics of this case, readers will learn to navigate the intricacies of trading around such corporate events.

Case Study 4: Regulatory Roadblocks In this case study, a biotech company encounters regulatory roadblocks that lead to delays in drug development. Traders will explore how regulatory setbacks can impact stock performance and market sentiment. By analyzing the challenges faced by the company in this case, readers will learn to assess the potential risks associated with regulatory hurdles.

Case Study 5: Navigating Market Volatility Market volatility is a constant in biotech trading. This case study delves into a scenario where a biotech trader navigates the volatility triggered by external factors such as macroeconomic events or geopolitical developments. Traders will gain insights into adapting trading strategies to manage risk and capitalize on opportunities amid market turbulence.

As readers immerse themselves in the depth of these case studies, they will emerge with a practical understanding of how strategies, principles, and considerations discussed throughout the book apply to real-world trading scenarios. By dissecting breakthrough designations, unexpected clinical trial outcomes, M&A deals, regulatory challenges, and market volatility, readers will be equipped to make informed trading decisions based on a comprehensive comprehension of biotech trading dynamics. As the journey through the world of biotech trading unfolds, subsequent chapters will continue to expand on specialized insights and strategies.

Chapter 17: The Future of Biotech Trading

The biotech sector is constantly evolving, driven by scientific advancements, regulatory changes, and market trends. Chapter 17 of "Biotech Trading: Navigating Biotechnology Stock Markets through Drug Development Insights" delves into the potential trajectories and considerations for the future of biotech trading, equipping readers to anticipate and adapt to the changing landscape.

Emerging Therapeutic Modalities: This chapter commences by exploring the potential of emerging therapeutic modalities such as gene therapies, cell therapies, and RNA-based treatments. Traders will gain insights into how these innovative approaches can reshape the biotech landscape and impact stock performance. By understanding the potential of these therapies, readers can identify investment opportunities at the forefront of scientific advancement.

Regulatory Landscape and FDA Evolution: The regulatory environment has a profound impact on biotech trading. This chapter examines how changes in regulatory policies, expedited review pathways, and FDA evolution can influence stock performance. Traders will explore how to stay attuned to regulatory trends and their potential implications for trading decisions.

Global Market Dynamics: Biotech trading is not confined to a single market; global dynamics play a pivotal role. This chapter delves into how factors such as international partnerships, market access, and healthcare policies can impact the performance of biotech stocks. Traders will gain insights into assessing the global landscape and its relevance to their trading strategies.

Influence of Big Data and AI: The integration of big data and AI continues to reshape biotech research and development. This chapter explores how AI-driven drug discovery, predictive modeling, and real-world data analysis can influence trading decisions. Traders will learn to leverage insights from data-driven technologies to inform their investment strategies.

Sustainable Biotech Investing: Environmental, social, and ethical considerations are gaining prominence in investing. This chapter examines how the concept of sustainable biotech investing is evolving and influencing stock performance. Traders will explore how to align their trading strategies with sustainable practices and evaluate the potential impact on long-term returns.

As readers delve into the intricate landscape of this chapter, they will emerge equipped with insights into the potential trajectories and considerations that will shape the future of biotech trading. By understanding emerging therapeutic modalities, staying attuned to regulatory changes, assessing global market dynamics, leveraging big data and AI, and embracing sustainable investing practices, traders will be primed to navigate the evolving biotech sector with foresight and adaptability. The journey through the world of biotech trading comes to a close, leaving readers with a comprehensive understanding of the intricacies and opportunities within this dynamic and innovative industry.

Chapter 18: Epilogue - Charting Your Biotech Trading Journey

In this epilogue of "Biotech Trading: Navigating Biotechnology Stock Markets through Drug Development Insights," we take a moment to reflect on the transformative journey you've undertaken through the pages of this comprehensive guide. As you stand at the crossroads of newfound knowledge and potential trading opportunities, this concluding chapter offers guidance on charting your biotech trading journey, emphasizing continuous learning, adaptability, and ethical responsibility.

Embracing Lifelong Learning: The world of biotech trading is dynamic and ever-evolving, shaped by scientific advancements, regulatory changes, and market trends. As you move forward, prioritize the pursuit of lifelong learning. Stay attuned to emerging technologies, industry shifts, and the latest research developments. Whether it's through scientific journals, market analysis, or expert forums, the commitment to staying informed will be your compass in navigating the complex biotech landscape.

Refining Your Strategies: The strategies and insights presented in this book serve as a solid foundation, but the journey doesn't end here. Take the time to refine and adapt your strategies based on evolving market conditions and your own experiences. Experiment with different approaches, evaluate their outcomes, and iterate to find what works best for you. Embrace both successes and setbacks as valuable learning experiences that contribute to your growth as a biotech trader.

Ethics as Your North Star: Ethical considerations lie at the heart of responsible trading within the biotech sector. As you make investment decisions, remember the profound impact that your choices can have on human health, well-being, and the broader society. Uphold ethical standards, avoid insider trading, and prioritize transparency. By integrating ethical considerations into your trading decisions, you contribute to the sustainability and integrity of the biotech industry.

Cultivating Resilience and Patience: Biotech trading, like any form of trading, is marked by ups and downs. The path to success is not always linear, and patience is a virtue. Cultivate resilience to weather market volatility and setbacks. Be prepared to adapt your strategies and adjust your expectations based on evolving circumstances. Remember that success often comes to those who persist with a long-term outlook and a steadfast commitment to learning from every experience.

Building a Network: In the realm of biotech trading, a strong network can be an invaluable asset. Connect with fellow traders, industry experts, and professionals who share your passion. Engaging in discussions, attending conferences, and participating in online forums can provide fresh perspectives, insights, and potential collaborative opportunities. Building a network can enrich your trading journey and expose you to a diverse range of viewpoints.

Contributing to the Biotech Community: As you navigate the biotech trading landscape, consider how you can contribute positively to the biotech community. Share your knowledge, insights, and experiences with others. Mentor aspiring traders, engage in discussions that promote responsible trading practices, and contribute to the collective understanding of the industry. By giving back, you not only enhance your own expertise but also foster a sense of shared growth within the community.

As you conclude this transformative journey through "Biotech Trading: Navigating Biotechnology Stock Markets through Drug Development Insights," remember that you are equipped with a wealth of knowledge, insights, and strategies to navigate the intricate biotech landscape. Embrace the challenges and opportunities that lie ahead, and let the lessons from this book serve as a steadfast guide as you chart your course in the ever-evolving world of biotech trading. Your journey is now in your hands, and your potential to make meaningful contributions to the field is boundless.

Conclusion

In the final chapter of "Biotech Trading: Navigating Biotechnology Stock Markets through Drug Development Insights," we reflect on the multifaceted journey undertaken through the pages of this book. The chapters have explored the intricate landscape of biotech trading, from the foundational understanding of drug development and clinical trial stages to the specialized strategies and ethical considerations that define success in this dynamic field.

As the biotech sector continues to evolve, propelled by scientific breakthroughs, regulatory shifts, and market trends, the knowledge gained from this book equips readers with the tools and insights to navigate the challenges and capitalize on the opportunities that lie ahead. The fusion of technical analysis, market sentiment, and ethical considerations has been meticulously woven together to provide a comprehensive guide for traders seeking success in biotech trading.

From the art of event-driven trading to the nuances of intellectual property evaluation, each chapter has unveiled a layer of expertise, guiding readers through the intricacies of a sector that melds science, finance, and human well-being. The case studies have brought theory to life, offering tangible examples of how strategies play out in real-world scenarios, and the exploration of emerging technologies and future trends has empowered readers to anticipate shifts in the market landscape.

The journey does not end with the last page of this book. Instead, it marks the beginning of a trader's path in the ever-evolving world of biotech trading. Armed with knowledge, insights, and a holistic understanding of the industry, readers are now poised to embark on their own trading journeys, making informed decisions that balance financial success with ethical responsibility.

As the biotech sector continues to push the boundaries of innovation, challenge conventions, and transform lives, those who have delved into "Biotech Trading: Navigating Biotechnology Stock Markets through Drug Development Insights" are well-prepared to contribute meaningfully to this remarkable journey. Whether as seasoned traders refining their strategies or newcomers entering the field, the knowledge gained from these pages will serve as a steadfast compass in the realm of biotech trading.

So, as we bid adieu to this comprehensive exploration, let it be known that the pursuit of success in biotech trading is not just a transactional endeavor—it's a holistic journey that balances the art of trading with the science of innovation, guided by ethical principles and a commitment to human welfare. May the insights garnered from this book illuminate your path and empower you to make impactful decisions in the captivating world of biotech trading.

Milton Keynes UK
Ingram Content Group UK Ltd.
UKHW021813010124
435297UK00016B/943